sparrow

Kelsi Rose

Winter Goose
PUBLISHING
where words take flight

Winter Goose Publishing
45 Lafayette Road #114
North Hampton, NH 03862

www.wintergoosepublishing.com
Contact Information: info@wintergoosepublishing.com

Sparrow

COPYRIGHT © 2016 by Kelsi Rose

First Edition, March 2016

Cover Design by Winter Goose Publishing
Typesetting by Odyssey Books

ISBN: 978-1-941058-40-4

Published in the United States of America

Contents

To my mother,
who gave me the seed of my strength,
who has watched me live and grow

Thank you for always believing in me

I have always been a writer. As a child, I would narrate my life as though it were my own personal story; even the most mundane of tasks were a great adventure. I have always told my own tales, weaving words into strings of imagery. This has always been completely normal for me.

When I was a preteen, I began my first love affair with poetry. From my very first poem, I have been continually growing, constantly changing my style and my words. I would say poetry was my first love, even before any boys came into my view. I have been dancing with it ever since.

The only way I can think to describe my writing is *molasses*. My writing is molasses. That sounds a bit odd to say, but it is slow, sweet, and a bit on the dark side. My inspirations are wildflowers and daydreams, but I also draw a lot of strength from who I've become and that factors into my writing quite a bit.

I am a product of my surroundings, having been victim to several parasitic relationships and friendships, having dwelled in a depression that ate away at my livelihood, having suffered in ways there are no words for, and having loved, having lived, and having found freedom in poetry.

Secret British Girls

Sometimes I stare at your picture for hours—remembering words you've never spoken aloud, remembering music you've never sung to me; the lyrics are just falling from the sky like rain and I am bathing in your beats. With these black-and-blue knees I'm kneeling at your feet, begging you to teach me how to fly. I never noticed you were simply a paper airplane, and that you'd crash—soon enough. And maybe you knew I'd just fail if I tried.

I am the salt on your skin in this air-dried ocean aria and I am the dirt under the nails of your work-worn hands. And tonight I locked myself away in this cedar chest, praying for discovery . . . and all the Magellans were bleeding roadmaps all over my lips with their compass tongues, just trying to find South. I watched pretty girls stumbling sleep-drunk through the bleeding pages of this novel, through the knothole in my wrist . . . and I'm waiting for a Soho sweetheart to whisper, "I couldn't. You'd just make fun of me," with a coy look and a lovely tongue sliding over her passive-aggressive lips. And I ached for her . . . wanting to slip myself into her silk-spun change purse like a love letter where she could circle my eyes like *Yes* or *No* and I could just fade into her red-light laugh.

Maybe I just read too much poetry, wasted too much time on search-and-rescue between the lines, looking for your smile. Because you told me some time ago that you had dropped it off the tallest buildings and the worst bridges as they were burning, and that you'd never expected to see it again. And I just wanted to see the stars return to your sky one last time before I faded into the city skyline like the thinnest fog. But I know you, and I know I will waste away on your bookcase like a novella you despised but hated to throw away just because, just because.

It's three a.m. somewhere, and I haven't slept and this aching in my bones just reminds me of you. Last night I left three notes on your windowsill telling you what kind of soul you had, I had. And why I'm no good for you, why you are not good for me. Did you notice? All those nights I was a ragdoll, begging you with my button eyes to tell me just how torn my seams were. All I asked for was the honesty, but honestly, I wish I had painted myself into your bed without you there. Into a hotel room, unoccupied, just waiting . . . just . . . waiting; a hooker, on her corner, who is twisting a Lucky 27 between her lips that are not so passive-aggressive this time. And she smiles before my camera as I zoom in on what's left of her sparrow heart, ripped apart like all those college letters she felt the need to destroy. She just couldn't afford the heartache. And now she's loving the cracks in the sidewalk a bit more affectionately, just hoping her stiletto doesn't get caught in its not-so-loving arms because that will be the end to her. She'd go spiraling down on her elbows and knees like a kid from a new bicycle and with her palms outstretched, she's grasping for you.

She's just asking for you, to beat her senseless. She's worthless, wearing as thin as those snagged stockings. She's got her eyes armed with fake tears for the day you decide she's not good enough, because one day, it won't really matter.

The moon is six shades of alabaster white and cream and gray, and it's just asking you to give yourself away, take a vacation and spend six months smoldering in his pocket like a good little dying star. It's the sorrow on your breath that makes me nauseated. That's the reason that I've curled myself against these porcelain portholes and emptied my emotions into the ocean waves. It's the reason I keep these bedside pills, to drown the hurt, to coddle the cuts until I've had time to heal and these heels, oh girl. They are biting blisters into your feet like hounds' teeth. I've got a fragment of a poem that says you were once beautiful before you sold yourself at yard sales for a fifty cent piece and a smile and I'm here to tell you to stop giving yourself away.

All these crumpled papers are screaming your name at me tonight. And I'm still awake if you're still willing to crumble like some sunbaked bumblebee on the bottom of the world, stuck under your shoe screaming, "I'm nothing, I'm nothing." You're an origami butterfly.

And I guess what I'm looking for is someone to tell me that you're real, that someone else has seen your mirage skin after thirty-eight hours awake and stumbling. I've got just enough words to keep me spitting like a jukebox, just keep feeding me your nickels. One. At. A. Time. And you can kick me when I say the wrong thing. Just as long as you keep me in your praying knees like bruises, I'll be faithless and follow you into your hysteria where the wisteria cling all whimsy to lattice fences. And sometimes, it hurts, to be so open-fleshed and beatable, when my skin is just so inviting to clenched fists and I am just so lovely to destroy. Bit by bit, I'm lovely. I could hang myself a million days in a million ways, and it would always make you smile.

Travelers

Your fingers,
wandering like vines of sweet pea,
curl passive around my waist,

come to rest on my hips
like weary travelers.

Tender, like your kisses,
I melt into your touch
with blooming, scarlet cheeks

Brittle Infinities

Small, my hands
in yours, dwarfed
and fervent;

I am eternal(ly)
aching
for your warmth

and your eyes
to consume me.

Il faut soffrir pour être belle; je n'ai pas assez souffert

"Faut souffrir pour être belle,"
but there is just nothing beautiful about it
and the river is so much uglier
than I like to pretend it is
with the weeds weaving their wild thoughts into my head
about how gorgeous nothing can be
and the shatter-boned corpses of trees,
naked brown skeletons with dry-rot for eyes,
blink at me and tempt me to sing to their driftwood flesh
in melodies only heartache can produce.
And I pine for the dandelions to blow me away,
for the mourning doves to drop me,
soaring on some abstract breeze,
for the termites to carve their labyrinth paths into my skin,

so I can feel again.

I stumble over the gnarled roots
of the guardians who shade me with their green-leaf coats,
with their arms stretched so high above their heads—I
breathe.
Kicking the smooth river stones
to the edge of the daffodil patches,
smiling at me with yellow teeth and swaying to the music
inside the oak trees,
breathing.

And I make bouquets of maple leaves and pinecones
with bluebells praying for the raindrops
to pitter-patter on my skin like Morse code,
to seduce the goosebumps into surfacing on my frail, sun
burnt arms,
to sink in.

And I drop sugar-tears for the ants and breadcrumb dreams
for the birds
as I shiver and sway against the pale day-dream breeze.
The leaves are tumbleweed dancers, pirouetting in the wind,
the same wind that abuses me, and kisses the bruises.

And the water stares at me with hard gray eyes,
telling me never to obsess over fantasy
because in the end, it just doesn't happen that way.
The sparrows echo thoughts so similar and
cut the sky with scissored wings—
but leave me sitting in bare rock thoughts,
with my faulty umbrella trees leaking the rain down on me
and all over my words,
painful and practiced as they are.
And there are no sunsets in loneliness
just as there is no beautiful moon to shine silver at midnight,
and I cannot live on high in the sun if it doesn't exist,
nor can I wake up the grass with a single kiss,
but the overcast clouds glare down on me to whisper
how pretty the suffering can be.

I am covered in mud-splattered aches,
in tulip bruises, in notebook clichés that render me

hopeless, stupid, spineless, and speechless.
And the river swirls into itself to remind me that
what is ugly can never become beautiful.
Even when the sky spits tears at my feet,
I fall as if they are glass
and whisper my prayers to a river goddess with wild tiger-
lily hair
and she tells me to hold on to my dreams,
fragile and pastel as they seem,
in the glittering light of her smile,
and that maybe one day, I'd shine despite myself.

Letters to Angels in Limbo

Dear boy,

I think of you often, more often as of late with the funerals taking up my fragile days. And I wonder; had you known I wore your very shoes that year, walked for miles until the sun blistered my china skin, would you still be hanging there—the memory of a painting that was ruined by careless hands. I ache for your presence, with only a vague skeleton of who you were, based on words I heard on a breeze; they came to me on dandelion seeds that caught in my hair and whispered secrets in my ear.

And dear boy, do you know how often I've tried to write this letter to you, how many paper angels have flown around my waste basket mourning you? Sighing, I am a ghost as always, but today I am pale and fragile; a paper cutout, wondering why origami cranes can't carry me to you so I can remember all those summer days I know there were; they are blank film negatives from the years where I consistently forgot to remove the lens cap.

Tonight, I am kicking myself for not knowing (you), for not trying harder; I could have saved you. I sit here writing you pseudo-beautiful things you can never read, but I know why now. I know why you committed suicide, dear boy. You wanted to fly and you were tired of being told no.

I understand, dear boy; I do. I just wish you would have taken me with you. You could have taught me how to fly like a sparrow on a strangled breeze, and finally, we would have been free.

I'm sorry for those days we threw stones and words, for the bruises and the breaks in our family ties, and for the distance that grew between us. You will always be the boy from down the street. I will always be the girl who listens for the trains. And we will always be a part of each other, no matter how many layers of atmosphere are between here and heaven.

I know; we always knew.

Fever-Sore

I read poetry
and remember that you don't love me,
and I try to sweat out a fever
that I can't fathom. My skin is warm
but the cold is in my bones
and I can't shake it;

not the way my hands shake
while I'm lifting teacups to my lips.

I am crashing.

I read poems that don't mean anything,
words I wrote when I was stupidly in love
with the thought of a boy whose hands were
my godsend. I remember that you don't love me.

I remember that he still does. I remember how it hurts
and how my heart breaks when I recall the bruises.

I read poems that were written for me.
Or about me, and I lose myself in thoughts of another life
where I never painted myself vulnerable and my lips
were as red as the blood on my wrists used to be.

Did you know the beeping of the thermometer
is faster, the higher the fever? I would know.

I've spent nights counting the degrees as they
climbed up like climbing vines. I am poetry.

I am fever-sore and you don't love me.

winterbones/summerskin

i.
I am winterbones and unsure hands,
eyelashes painted black and poem pieces like paper maché,
smile-shy and secret-colored eye,
lips like loneliness.
I am broken words and snowflake skin,
fragile thoughts past three a.m.,
and freckles that dot my nose like dust spots.

I was made for you to love me,
to kiss my February lips;
to melt me into mud puddles.
I was made to bury myself in your summerskin
with your knowing fingers tangled in my hair,
as lost and sunken as shipwrecks.
And I was meant to shine for you,
to be your north star
to follow until your hands found their way
to the small of my back,
until your lips found my lips.

I was looking for a lighthouse,
looking for an anchor,
anything to keep me from drifting out to sea
with bed sheet sails and ocean eyes.
I found your smile sparkling as a treasure thing
and I kept you inside my heart

like a secret I might never speak of,
a caged bird singing,
songs like sonnets.

I am a snowstorm,
a white-on-whiteout,
frozen bits of flowers
kissed frosted like your windowpanes
and melting like candle wax
under your tender fingers.

You are my summer sun . . .

ii.
You are soft smiles and certain fingers,
sun-painted skin and wounded eyes,
broad-back'd and stable-spined;
your wonderfully wandering mind
and the curve of your lips.

You are a stranded star,
warmth that spreads on my skin
like a wildfire
or a flush that blooms across my cheeks.
You melt me faster than wax wings,
leave me breathless
and weak-knee'd,
ready to fall into your open arms.

You were made for me to love you,
to cherish the scent of your skin
and the sound of your laugh.
You were made to weave your limbs into my limbs
until we are just a tired mess
in tangled sheets,
skin-on-skintimacy,
and I am breathing in your spirit.

You are something special, a light
that I've only ever seen flash from the corner of my eye;
the electricity that builds up
in static shocks and thunderstorms,
the energy that breaks through clouds.

You are the rain, the summer sky water
that I've been praying for in this drought,
and I am soaking in your love.

Aching

i.
I just want
a ribcage full of thistle,
a handful of brambles caught up in my hair;

want to run wild, my heart
beating and aching as a hummingbird's love song,
want to tell the stars that they can't fall

hard enough,
or fast enough
to fade unnoticed.

I want breaking mornings, sleeping blue
and sonorous, your voice in my thoughts
at my waking moments.

ii.
I am aching to the rhythm of your breath,
delicate and dreaming.
Darling, this is what love feels like:

to be the space between kisses,
the tension between two sets of skin
with soul-mate symptoms.

I just want to be
your every daydream dissolved into reality,
a rush of endorphins and a laugh
that makes your heart
stop short.

iii.
I want to stay up, to watch you sleep,
your soft-spoken breath, the rise and fall of your chest
beneath me, and sometimes,

your heartbeat to lull me to
a place where words have no meaning,
where emotions speak like lyrics,
like laundry lists of what I love
about you, about us.

I am arched backs,
like little bridges,
tangled fingers like
telephone lines,
and I am resting
in your roses.

Hungry Mouths

I tremble,
like nervous fingers
as you count the freckles on my skin
and draw in constellations,
and kiss between my shoulder blades
to close the gaps between vertebrae,

and your mouth is hungry,
eating away the spaces where my spine
does breathe, and where does the shuddering end,
if not your lips?

Pastel Pale

I yawned away my childhood,
always wanting, always ready to grow
up, and older, and out of my skin;
shed myself like a snake,
and leave just a memory
with the dust and the dreams,
and the stuffed animals I'd deemed
too young for me.
I read books—many, many books,
voraciously and tenderly
and I read a thousand words a minute;
every time, I took a step forward.

Years are slow, except to those who reminisce
on past lives, powdered noses, rosy knees.
Yesterday, I was a child, still a child,
a broken bit—threadbare skinned,
weakened but stronger, and stronger.

I am a girl-child emblazoned with magician's eyes,
able to disappear like white rabbits, reappear
like white doves; I am always white,
but not pure, not chaste.

The Sparrows

There are sparrows building nests of twigs and heartstrings
of star-sparks and dead flowers, of birthday wishes and
melted candles
on the inside of my ribcage,
hidden in the crevices where I once buried my insecurities,
the dark place where I used to keep
the sound of my guarded laugh
and the good dreams that melted
into something sickly sweet,
the faint sound of a heartbreak,
the fragility of a smile;

sparrows.

They start singing at the idea of dawn,
at first, just murmurs,
whispers in the dark of five a.m.,
with my heart as a backbeat
a noise that grows with the first breaths of the morning.
I am born with the sound of the birdsong
beating through my turquoise veins,
dancing like a dandelion meets breeze,
child's breath,
freeing prisoners into a free place,

the air.

Lungs aching, eyes filled up with the thoughts of you,
tiny little teardrops like birdbaths.
Laughter—like a splendid thing,
echoing in the chasm, falling back into a happy place
where sun-sparkling eyes breathe life
into deadlings,
birds with broken wings
buried in ribcage graves.

I leave flowers on my skin
dried, blown away like chipping paint
from the windows of your soul
pressed pastel, memoirs of old Hollywood
and places we've never been
smiling through a clock face,
dreams wiped away from the corners
of your tired eyes,
lullabies on mangled mobiles.

Sparrow songs that sound like beachside carousel calliope,
wild horses dancing like falling stars
wearing Mardi Gras masks and a bruised dream.

Seashells and singing things,
sunspots tattooed to the insides of eyelids,
you'll see the sun even when your eyes are closed,
memories burnt into skin
the way white notebook paper curls into smoke,
into smoldering dreams that you hold in your fingers
like the neck of that aching violin,
strung taut strings and a crying voice.

A sparrow pressed to the inside of your spine
like a spring flower,
preserving the song between the pages of
books bound in leather like a second skin.

I bury dreams in bones
like treasures,
bird nests and breadcrumbs.

Playground

A swing-set to the sun,
flying high with gravity
tickling in her stomach.

She's so carefree with her unlaced shoes
streaking through the sky like rockets,
rocking in rhythm . . .

.back.
    .and.
.forth.

She flies.
She flies so far before she falls
and shatters into so many pieces of herself.

With her merry-go-round thoughts
spinning haphazardly,
she holds her stomach,
suppressing the vomit
as it dances in her throat.
She looks stupid when she smiles.
You don't have to tell her.
She already knows.

She's so simple.
She's so plainly, nonchalantly,
a glance-over-the-shoulder beautiful.
But she doesn't know it, not with her child's mind.
She thinks so openly, so averagely, so . . . things we never see—
like smoke on the mountain and lady bug eyes, hidden
treasures that she catches
in her swirling hair, leaves and lost thoughts, clovers and
three a.m. coffee shops
that cater to insomniac nymphs who don't need the caffeine.

She dances across the macadam, burning her bare feet.

The blistering sun, her blushing skin, the freckles that spin
all out of control and chaotic across her nose. And it just
goes to show, it doesn't matter who raised her, because she'll
always be a free spirit.

I could do so much more with her mind,
but I'd have to break her, and I'm not sure I could stand
to see her eyes look at me with that kind of pitiful glint
that only broken girls can produce. I couldn't stand that
quivering bottom lip.

She balances see-saws, pretending to be a tightrope walker,
walking waywardly onto highways with an empty can
perched perfectly on her head, and never faltering.

Even under the sweltering heat, she smiles.
Sweat drops magnifying her freckle features, her pigtails braided down her back, dandelions wound around her fingers like wedding bands.

She is a child,
an orchid, sipping sunlight.
She swings her way to happiness,
chains rattling as she tastes the sky.
She says it tastes like freedom.

Courtesan

"Sex sells," he tells her, tallying up the numbers
of boys who fell at her feet, worshipping her as a goddess;
the number of boys she's pushed away, broken-hearted
and gasping for their final wishes on stars that she kept on
leashes.

She sighs . . .

But she knows no other way; knows no other opportunity
to grasp for, to gasp for. She knows no stars to pine for, no
pines to wish for, no wishes worth her subdued lust . . . No
men worth her trust.

And he nods, grinning through jack-o'-lantern teeth. He is
her cotton candy sanity, pulled thin and wispy, sugarcoated
cavities. He is the way she thinks and speaks and the way
the words curl like the embers at the end of her cigarette.
And she wants to breathe without a car crash tangling up
her vocal cords, to sleep with silence in a place where the
lilacs grow and suffocate the sudden splintering of voices.

She wants . . .
Oh, God, how she wants . . .
Wants the sun to rise golden, pink, and mandarin, with
amethyst clouds—dreaming wishes. She wants to lie in
open arms, holding her heart close.d

She asks for love with just her eyes;
eyes that tremble beneath her eyelids just briefly when she blinks,
like twin bumblebees encased in silk eyelid ever lilies.

With your broad back and your stable spine, she hopes you can support her
wilting flower thoughts. With your lattice lies building her up, she's in love.

But how could she be—how can a creature of the night, lovely and young and beautiful as she (hopes she) is, pull herself from an emotional war that she's been fighting for nearly two decades?
She is nothing, if not a disorder.

She.
is.
nothing.

"I'm where you want to be . . ." she whispers, ". . . but never where you are."

And she closes the pages of her bleeding heart, to keep the ink from running off the page, touching hearts of poet-boys and men who understand love.

Because she doesn't.
    She never could.

            Some days, she's afraid she never will.

Demons

She couldn't recall

where she was on a night blessed by a rain so fresh that it caused the wilted flowers to rise up on their toes in excitement, and her to wither into her depression. The night was a lightning-show of blue-white flashes from a thousand cloud cameras.

And the gravel beneath her feet was simply the degraded souls that she had put down on nights before this one, souls that she had torn from her spine like vertebrae and left to rot into something resembling what she felt inside.

The rain could never wash away
the smell of her sk.incense.

And today was no different, so she drowned herself in rose petals and broken glass, just so she could suffer in beautiful elegance. The freckles on her shoulders were the pinprick memories she insisted on forgetting, the forever-after tally-mark scars documenting how often she was horrid;

millions

of gold flecks in her eyes, because secretly, she's always been a bit of a gold-digger and it's just her soul's way of showing her true colors.

Gold-digger and envy-green marbles that quiver in the light of the rising sun,
with her pupils dilating in ink-based agony. And the sound of her heart vibrating in her ears with that horrible hiccupping rhythm she had grown to hate causes her to shake in an anxious anticipation.
And it means nothing.
It couldn't possibly.
She lives in her memories, torn at the edges of the filmstrip clubs and the dirty little secrets that she forces between her lips. A kiss.

She's such a . . .
faded thought.

Lost in translation. She's (a) patient with her medications calling home in the middle of the night
to say she missed you.

But never as much as you missed her (mind).

And she's quite queer,
dangling star-of-Davids from her collarbone
and a set of rosary beads in her pocket.

Just trying to cast out the demons,
just trying to cast new people for the parts of this play;
she's just playing.

Act(ing)
natural.

Because it's so much easier to smile
than to explain those dreaded tears
falling off her face (of the earth).

She falls
(fails)

and withers once more,
a tumbleweed
who is far too fragile.

Who could resist
trying to break her?

                                        No, I never could.

Confession / Depression

I am from an ugly town in a valley where the air is pure and smells not unlike those scented candles on your peel-paint windowsill. And the flowers in my hair are picked from wild fields, shot up between patches of blow-away dandelion liars and bare-thorn briars, and grown by no one's gentle hand but the wind and the rain and the smiling sun that cringes beneath your smog.

I can hardly breathe here.

So I hold my breath until I'm blue in the lips and red in the face, till the whites of my eyes nearly pop from my head. And despite it all, I am breathlessly patriotic, even when I don't want to be. I've got my qualms about leaving my ugly, three-tone house lined by a crooked white fence, a pond, and grass that grows too quickly; a yard eaten and overwhelmed by bulging tomato vines and azalea that the puppy will gnaw on, vomit, and then gnaw again.

And I must say, I admire her commitment, how she comes back day after day with the same goofy smile wired into her jaw, and why can't I do that? We're not so different, after all, but only in words do I truly live. She cannot speak in a common language—and I'm too tired to learn hers.

And this is not so much a poem as it is a confession because I am a bad pearl caught in an oyster's mouth, like food between its teeth. And I thrive in the swirls of smoke from a cigarette dancing on stagnant air as if it were center stage.

I am from a tiny town you've never heard of, mostly because I've never mentioned it. It tastes so bittersweet on my tongue that I cringe to vocalize it—it sounds so very much like it is: small, cramped, and racist. And there is no fun in these honeysuckle woods, where only girls like I could grow—an imposter; a redneck, blue collar, white-skinned imposter of American beauty. This is not who I am.

I am a sun kissed pearl dressed in jaundiced paper dresses with my hair tied back in ribbons that fray at the ends. I have been wearing the same shoes for over a year now, not because they are still in good condition—they've worn thin and holey, with rips and tears and torn rubber (it gives them character)—but because I can't part with my packrat history and I'd hate to lose the memory. My body aches—perhaps worn thin like these shoes too often feel. And this, truly, is not a poet speaking softly to her paper.

I count ceiling tiles too many times because I always forget the exact number, and sometimes I cannot finish because my mind wanders off to play like a small child—and I am left a shell of what I am, with no conscious thoughts to guide my hands. They are covered in pseudo-bruises, remnants of painted days where I used to thrive, but can no longer.

I kick dandelions with these worn out chucks that were never waterproof but are less-so now with holes rotting into their soles and teeth biting at their laces and, I will never truly be an All-Star . . . but I wish like hell that I could be. I wish on a hundred dandelion seeds kicked silent into the breeze that I breathe so openly because there's air here in this perfectly ugly valley.

I am cradled between train tracks and a river bed—one aggravated and one perfectly calm . . . and you'd never know which is which unless you have lain on the tracks at midnight or sat at the water's edge in a storm—tempting fate. Just waiting for something to do you in, so you don't have to.

Stumbling

"You cannot sleep
because you haven't tried,"
said the white rabbit to the dream-girl.
"Haven't you noticed *tried* and *tired*, they're very close indeed.
And I know because the sleep cannot come
when you're so fish-eyed awake.
So close your eyes and spin your dreamcatcher,
you tiny, invalid arachnid and fall
into a beaded wonderland of polka dotted skies
and cracked turtle shell realities."

And the dream-girl stared
wide and walleyed at a speaking rabbit,
checking the time on his pocket watch wishes.

Seeing can only be believing
when we believe we are dreaming.

"I am no Alice with my Cheshire cat smile
fading into the stars,"
she said so matter-o'-factly that her voice
nearly echoed in his ears.
"And what of the mercury-maddened hatters
sipping cyanide-laced tea.sing me into trying
some liquid nightmares
to stop these bitter jackhammer thoughts.
J-j-j-ust break.king up the madness and blowing kisses

to the queen who was never lovely . . .
lying passed out in a blurred motel room,
in God knows where,
with her crown tilting and tipping drunkenly from her head
in the most degrading way,
all the while crying,

"I am pretty!"
But she's petty at best.

And she beats me with her overly punctuated whiskey
words,
and in quiet desperation I pray to her city with a quivering
breath,
holding on to the thought of a Hookah Express vacation
that I so long ago booked a ticket for but have since misplaced.

Miss.placed, am I, in this cold-spun dreamer world
where the typewriters type love letters in poetic displays of
y.our affection.

And they pile on your pillows—day after day—like hotel
mints and clean, bleach-white towels to bury your face in
while you're rambling on in metaphors and references
to things I can never quite place.
I place my words so delicately upon your painted lashes and
inked lips
while you sleep (though you're never silent).

And you're so lovely an everlily, silken skin polished alabaster
glow.

You are virtually as invisible as you feel
against the freckled sky and tiger lilies with their cancer-
spot eyes that never wilt. And never close because someone's
always watching when you're sinning so religiously."

Tick.tick. tock.

The watch flicks milliseconds like a time bomb,
milking you for your every last breath
like a divine bovine.
You're just an animal, baby.
And we're all so mad here, with our pharmaceutical,
therapeutical techniques giving us spots to count when the
sheep have all gone to pasture and left us sleepy-eyed but
mind-awake in cold sheets absent of wool.

And here we are, sprawled across ourselves because we know
not how else to be, and we can't consider the consequences
of cuddling with cigarettes and razorblades
because no one cares when the moon strikes midnight. Like
a match made in heaven
and this is the wedded bliss of insanity and magnolia blossoms
kissing sweet the wind with their potent perfumed tongues.
And laughing far too loudly in a room that's grown silent
like ladies who are blissfully unaware of how boisterous
their voices are.
Like ladies. And we hold open doors wide for their auras to
fit through because they are so radiant even without their
cracked tiaras—with spoiled diamonds falling like stars that
we'll drown in. They are so radioactively radiant, dancing in
the rain with their braids dripping rivers down their clavicle

valleys and their painted toes dug into the mud, masking the effort of their beauty, because they are so beautiful covered in angel tears.
And muddled minds think alike.

I'd like to hold that tiny Ace of Hearts.haped faces
and take her places
on my feathered wings,
just so she can finally know how it feels to

.fly.

Ocean Eyes

Ocean girl,
choking on jetsam and shipwreck debris, drowning in the words that drunken sailors slur into the storm; your jeans are too tight, you bright little starfish; suffocating your spindly legs in denim and dreams.

And your shell's too cold, a beautiful clam, because you keep yourself so closed and barren when the bottom-feeders feed on the shattered vertebrae from the broken-spined girls with crushed hopes who lie empty-eyed in the sand.

"I'd rather be an ugly mermaid, than a beautiful riptide, with my kelp and coral hair clinging to my shoulders like your hands when you're holding me back."

Dear, you're too potent to be so precious and your sea foam eyes are my safe harbor. Please let me anchor myself into you . . . You're such a safe bet, and a bad dream that I'd hate to wake from, purely for the reason of knowing how you end. And it's only entertainment, love; because you're so much cheaper than cable bills and porno subscriptions. And forty thousand leagues under the sea, you are somebody's wet dream—you almost have to be.

With your seashell palms dripping with fake pearls, you are so falsely lovely. And you are so undeserving of love, I know you feel it in your seahorse spine because of the way you fall forward and crumble in the sand—and I know you speak purely for the sake of the conversation, not the art, because your tongue isn't capable of being that flexible.

And blink

your colorblind eyes underwater. The saltwater burns but only as much as your own tears. Nothing more, just enough to destroy your sandcastle confidence when you're so choked up in seaweed nooses and you keep coughing up what's left of your smile, no longer pearlescent but waterlogged lovely.

Just lovely.
Your sea-skin is plagued by barrier-reef bruises, with goosebumps, it loses its pallid luster, and then, drowned in metaphors and lost in sunken ships, we use the last of our oxygen on each other; confessing our souls in silent air bubbles until our lungs ache for love.

Waiting.
Knowing one of us will die before we surface. And I'm so lightheaded, floating upwards
just waiting to hear her scream
but fearing she'll fall silent.

And it's the silence that would kill me, to not hear her crushed saline words as they fall from her eyes and drown me in a way that's far more painful. But always worth it.

Almost

Sometimes she liked to think that you were the story written to keep her from killing herself, not because when she read you, she found a little more of herself inside your dog-eared corners, but because even though she knows you aren't there to keep her breathing, it always brings comfort to her frightened soul on the nights where she sweats herself to sleep.

And it's so hot tonight
despite the fan, that she's practically begging to take off her skin for you. To bare it all and show that she isn't as afraid as she used to be. She's so fully-prepared to lie to you because she knows that under the shadow of lust, you won't care if she's ready or not (and here you come).

And it won't matter, because she'll try her hardest to bite back her tears, knowing that there comes a point when she'll realize she's too pretty for the way you treat her. But that point is miles and miles and millions of magnolia blossoms away tonight. And her skin is so silkily inviting to your fingers that you just can't help yourself and she won't stop you. Because she is the softest leather and the smoothest porcelain and deep down, she knows she's beautiful.

But on the surface, she's so insecure and broken that she wonders if her eyes look like jagged, green-glass bottles; like the ones that wash up on her riverfront, shore-line sanctuary and she wonders just how eerily jaundiced her skin looks in the light of the setting sun. She shivers, forcing herself to focus, because even though she hates it, she just wants to make you happy.

The story never changes, because she's too fragile to make the first move. And so you leave her, feeling beaten down and nauseated with whatever path you've chosen for her. And she'll never be as happy as she was when she was dying.

I swear to God, she was almost free.

.

Lunatics and the Color Red

My body is so sore, it hurts to be touched, to be held, to walk myself up creaking stairs with my creaking bones and tender muscles and please . . . don't touch me. I can't bear the thought of cringing from your nimble fingers and I'd hate to see you hurt me when there's so much time left on the clock. And you know, it hurts to smile too brightly because subconsciously we know we're not meant to.

We're not meant to smile with the eyes of our dead ancestors twinkling like stars, like so many millions of cracked diamonds dusting the skies like a freckle-faced ginger.

And I speed-read poetry, searching for kick start inspiration though I can never stutter words so beautifully with this broken pen, bleeding out in black-and-blue. I sink to my knees, bruised purple like exotic wildflower kisses, and the sounds of the river make me shiver so violently.

I cry.
No one can know the reason . . . it's just too big of a weight to throw at them, and I can't even lift it. I cannot speak it. And it carries the power to break every one of you into what I am.

So what if you love my mind—I only show you the pieces that I know won't cause you to shatter because I'm too tired to gather all the pieces and put them in my pockets.

But the birds know, they always have known about my inner-cynic thoughts perhaps because I spend far too much time whispering to the wind, who can't keep a secret anyway.

And it's all about girls with star tattoos on their wrists and tiger lilies on their hips because they're the ones who will blink without a second thought as to what they're closing their eyes to; who don't pose every statement as a question to avoid sounding too opinionated (like I do), and they are the broken things that have made you cry like the rain on the evening of some warm summer night and the birds crying in your bookcases about the bumblebees hibernating in your teacups. Like the spilt milk on your marble counters and your marbles spilled all over the floor, scattering—
And words are overrated.

Speaking is no more an art than crying but at least the words can frame you into something beautiful.

Something beautiful.
Like realizing you are interesting
after the suicide attempts burn your skin and the scars are a million smiling faces, smiling like you ought to, and the snowflakes in your static-mind are Post-it notes on ecstasy, swirling around your head like a snow globe in a blizzard-state. Like the dead streets that call your name to lie in them in the moonless night and the panicked thoughts that leave you so stressed that you have no choice but to

laugh at yourself. Because you know it doesn't matter. And you know there's nothing like holding a smoldering cigarette between your fingers and not smoking it, just because you don't have to.

And there's nothing like the chill of an empty stomach to keep you going, to keep you showing that you've not given up just yet and that you won't go down without a damn good fight. With this paper doll army, you'd think we couldn't lose.

But it's the girls with the curves who call the shots, nowadays. And we fade into each other with heads hung in absolute disgust and our self-loathing thoughts turn towards each other and we've lashed out with our own whips.

And even with our blind eyes, we can see how hating ourselves drives everyone else away and we are hookers and drug dealers and princesses with broken tiaras and birds with broken wings who still try to sing the same songs as the girls on TV.

And I have no star tattoos; I left my tiara in Atlanta, trying hard to spit my poetry like watermelon seeds onto my paper. But it's all about pressure points and falling down and the sorrys we whisper in the dead of night when we think no one can hear them. Because there's no one there to listen.

But maybe we can make a wish on a falling feather
and fall together
until we're just a mess of broken bones and bloody noses
on the concrete, bleeding raindrops and sidewalk chalk
thoughts, heads like pomegranates burst open and staining
all our eyes red.

And won't that just be lovely.

Dandelion Dreams

She breathes in that awful, nostalgic scent of attics and memories and dried flowers that hang from the tilting rafters like bats—breathes the musty air into her cracked ceramic lungs and bleeds dry like terra cotta flowerpots.

And she slumps backwards like a ragdoll with her stuffing pulled out, so forlorn and button-hungry. She sighs so heavily, dropping her shoulders as if they weigh a million pounds . . . and she can just barely hold them up again.

She spends her better days like this.

Dreaming in dust clouds and white lace wedding dresses, blue-China tea-sets, and beauteous mink coats draped over broken rocking chairs; but not dreaming at all—just simply seeing with past-tired eyes, just simply sleeping with her dried out, white and bloodshot-pink, oleander eyes wide open. She swallows moths and hidden treasures in attempts to remind herself where she came from, and where these memories were birthed like so many dreams.

And remember she does.

Once, she was a sunflower child in a paisley dress, drooping on cracked pavement dreams, wilting and tilting under the pressure of the cruel summer sun, bruised by the dirty hands of ashen children who meant to break her. And on many days they did and she lay burning on the sidewalk in agony, counting the sunspots as they ate her eyes.

And once, when she was wilting on the side of the street, hugging her knees to her fragile, fragile chest, he saw her. She was crying tears that cut her face in the glaring white of day and her hair was braided with dandelions and fell over her shoulders like bits of rope—

and he thought of how preciously beautiful she appeared to be, with her shoes melting into the asphalt, rooting her into the street, stealing away her smile.

But he couldn't see how perfectly broken she was, even then; just a little girl waiting to fall in front of some unsuspecting car and wondering if they could stop in time, but she doubted they could and that was what kept her rooted on the yellow curb, kicking gravel into the storm drains and listening to her mother's voice, played on loop inside her head, reminding her to not play in the street.

And once, she was a pyromaniac princess, burning butterflies with glowing match sticks, and pretending to be God, with her dandelion halo perched on her head like a crown. She was beautiful and dangerous—in the most harmless way, because you knew that if she found a broken heart, she would spend hours on it, as if it were but a simple puzzle, putting it back together; and she would collect them on her bookshelves like the treasures that would one day clutter her attic.

And he saw her once, crouched low to the ground with a magnifying glass in one hand, manipulating the sun. The anthill was chaos beneath her fingers, which made her feel powerful, even when the dandelions were falling free of her tangled hair and littering their graves.

Now, sitting chest-deep in her musty memories, with her childhood persona whispering over her shoulder, she wonders where she went and when her aching bones became so brittle.

"Where have the years gone?" she whispers to the room. "And what of the dandelions, have they all withered and blown away in the wind?"

Philadelphia

Philos adelphos.
The City that Loves You Back,
Quaker City, Cradle of Liberty;
Active, dodgy, warfare.

The City of Brotherly Love:

They tell me you are iniquitous and I believe them, for I
have seen
your beautiful crack-whores dying under the streetlight
haloes.
And they tell me you are a criminal and I answer:
"Perhaps,
but I have seen your drug dealers stealing innocence in the
thriving after-hours of the city
and in comparison, perhaps you are not so bad."
And they tell me you are a brutal killer, and yet I reply:
"Yes, but
she is as fair as a disease; she does not discriminate."
They tell me you are immoral, impure, and unjust
and with tears glinting in my eyes, I reply: "Yes, but she's
mine."
Having defended you, I turn my back on them and
challenge them
with the words I whisper under my breath:
"Find me a beautiful city free of violence and with no
dying

prostitutes littering the street corners.
Find me the beauty in little towns that breed their suicides
like manicured rosebushes in the white-fence wonderland
of suburbia.
Find me the rival gangs that share a meal and break bread
together; you can't.
Singing bullets shattering through storefront upon
storefront, here
where the buildings stab at the sky like shivs;
the eyes as glaring as broken glass and just as pointed, the
soft comfort between strangers
is shattered and estranged.
Building,
advancing,
developing,
fighting, striving, winning."

Under the stray streetlight pools of yellow, her hair tangled
in a disagreement
with the wind, smiling from lips so robustly red.
Under the pressure of apathy and agony, smiling like it
would keep the world spinning,
smiling even though the night sky is obscured in smog,
masking the beautiful pin-prick stars
who had always won her heart,
murmuring and smiling about the dreams she lives out
here,
the freedom, ignoring the pain of this poverty-stricken
paradise.
Smiling!
Smiling passed the active, dodgy warfare of guns and

gangsters, pimps and prostitutes,
drugs and cold, hard cash—filthy money that slips
between your fingers,
loves you, smiles at you; philos adelphos: The City That
Loves You Back, The Quaker City, Cradling Liberty.

Love and Confidence

His work-worn hands
stitched a spine,
vertebrae by precious vertebrae,
into my paper.back
and he told me to feel beautiful;
the gasping stars were envious of my eyes.
He whispered iloveyous
into the windswept strands of my hair
and kissed each ugly thought
until it became something lovely again.
And then, I was born again, too,
as a beautiful afterthought of what I once was,
with my hollowed voice
echoing off the starlit sky
and my lips
kissing his,
dreams until the moon
drowned itself on the horizon of my mind.
I wept for it,
allowing him to weave
his workman's fingers through my hair
and sew the stars
into my eyes.

Inconsolable

There are some deaths so surreal
that even after hospitals, funerals, and mourning,
you still don't believe.

And on those nights,
half-asleep,
your thoughts turn to them
and you can still hear their voice inside your head
paired with images of ashes in urns,
funeral bouquets,
and white tissue thoughts dabbing the tears from your eyes.

And there's something about seeing a grown man

cry

that is just so debilitating
that you can't control yourself.

So you don't.

You rub your nightmare eyes
until they're the rawest red in color
and the sunlight makes them itch.

Though there's no use in crying,
you do

until you can't breathe and
someone pulls you into their bosom
to console you . . .

And you only cry harder.

Genophobic

..
She is a (weeping) willow
ending her seventeenth summer

and she is horribly,
deathly
afraid

of what lies dormant
in your grass.

..

Pessimism

I am the storm cloud
on the horizon,
coughing raindrops
because I can't vomit silver-sequin linings
like you do.

Love: An Interpretation

I thought on a dream,
        on a whim,
                on a whisper
and I stayed because there was no one left
to listen.

I couldn't entertain the idea of the wind being lonely
so I lay breathing and breaking in the fields of white flowers
waiting for you
to speak

and your words broke like white waves,
crashing on me
as my heart sank a little deeper in my chest.

I love you.

As the thought leaves my lips,
your eyes turn from me
and you smile into the sun.

She Said No.

She
(unlike a lot of pretty girls,
who couldn't resist
the temptation in your eyes
when you told her she was beautiful)
scoffed.
And when you tried to convince her . . .
she punched you lightly
on the arm
and told you
to stop making fun of her
because the jokes had lost their tastes
like gum does.
She popped a bubble between her teeth
with her mascara-bare eyelashes
dusting off her cheekbones,
she's never seemed so wilted
this star-sick lily
but her petals fold around her eyes like tears.
She forces herself into hibernation

mid-spring.

Ten-Line Tragedy

Salt water words,
the voice of the ocean,
she spoke from her eyes,
amplified only by the drop of her lashes
and the curve of her cheek.
She wrote poetry with her tears,
beautiful tragedies
of storm clouds with silk spun thread
and thunder like the voice of God,
calling, calling . . .

Pretenders

Your wings look like spilled ink
and the way you stare
into your coffee makes me nervous.
What are you thinking?
And after we exhale
the limelight burns my eyes.
I see sunspots like Rorschach,
the shapes, ruptured like your memory.

I lick my lips
chapped, swollen,
and there's broken glass in my coffee cup.
Bleeding,
too calm like a dream,
too calm to be reality.
Smile.

A broken half-hearted crescent
and the sparrows know you're crooked;

pretending like children do,
we fold out tongues over our words,
saving each other
by hiding from ourselves.

Who will we be tomorrow?

Love Is a Smoldering Cigarette

You(r words)
made my cheeks burn red
like the embers of the cigarettes

you never smoked,

but liked to cradle between your fingers
when mine were too far away
to be entwined with yours.

Like Vultures, Love. Like Vultures

She was a bedroom poet
with black and blue eyes
who cringes at the butterf.lies
you tainted with your touch.

You spelled out her secrets
in the smoke rings
she wrapped so deftly around her finger,

and she coughed delicate sounds
as she
r e a c h e d

to kiss the stars in a marbled sky.

She fell at your feet,
this beautiful mess
and vomited metaphors,

whispering how the stardust
choked her
and how the constellations ate her voice
like vultures.

Waking Thoughts

Do you remember her waking up in his arms
and his lips moving to the words
"I love you"?

Do you remember her eyes smiling and her laughter
. . . like ice cubes in cold glass?
She'd grown up
to be such a beautiful disaster.

Do you remember when he became her shelter?
Her father beat her spirit until she lay
shaking on the concrete,
cradling fallen stars and whispering,
"We're not meant to smile."

He held her like she'd break again
and met her whispers with reciprocated promises
and he spoke of better things.

She slipped between broken glass and dirty laundry
with eyes like oceans and starless skies
and she'd never looked more beautiful than she did
the night where all she did was bite her lip
and stifle her screams.

Do you remember the black shadows around her eyes
when she was too afraid to sleep
because the bruises might not fade?

Static

I have been likened to e e cummings for the poetry that I occasionally write in the lines in my palms . . . I don't know why. I have been compared to both women and young girls, to a good soul, to bad weather. to a sunset. to a death. I have been told I look like a desperate interpretation, an open heart (surgery), a fingerprint on a pane of stained glass.

I have been called a church, a lady, a failure, and a nightmare dressed in a plaid skirt with pigtails that fall off my shoulders. I am a sketch, a snow globe, a single firefly looking for its mate. I have never caught a wedding bouquet . . . mostly because I do not go to weddings; I find them far too sad. Girls like me, we know. We know too often and far too well that we don't belong in eternity. No kiss could be worth that loss of freedom.

I am an old, old woman with the innocence of an eight-year-old girl, from a time when children didn't sleep with strangers for drug money. And every day I get older; every day I die a little in the creases of my brown-leather home. I haven't left my couch in weeks, you know. Today, I read too much Bukowski . . . and my eyes began to burn. like candles, white wax candles.

I tuned my radio to a station that played only faint static . . . the bags under my eyes were far too heavy, so I popped an aspirin between the drunken texts of a man who was falling harder than he should, a man who couldn't see that I was broken luck. He fell in love with my suffering. And I kept suffering so he would keep loving me, but I've been hoping you'd call. How long has it been? How many moonless nights have I lain naked without your breath on my skin? My guess is far too many. And him? Well, he's a poor substitute for a firefly.

"You don't need a name," he whispers. "It's just another lie."

I have been drinking from the same Pepsi can for going on seven hours now. It's room-temperature flat, no carbonation to tickle my nose; I like it better that way. It distracts me less than something I might like. I dropped my smile . . . off the boulevard. off the pier over the too-calm, gray-green-black water—like tears and c.old mascara. with the seagulls scraping for boardwalk fries. The clouds I keep my head in are pregnant with rain and bursting silver lining seams. It must be a wedding day.

"One day, you'll pay for brilliance like this . . ."

But for tonight, enjoy the thought of me, remember me as perfect as you thought I was, though(t) we both knew better. I am a street sign and a trafficked highway, complete with red lights. I am a cherry-flavored sucker, a fractured shadow, a girl who thinks too much. A girl who loves her notebook more than any man, who takes it to bed with her every night, sleeps in its inked arms, shares every waking thought . . . and several ones when she's asleep. But I only write poems for you. That's one victory you can always walk away with.

Cirque du Sept (Perhaps an Epic)

Seven imaginary girls dance silhouette solos inside a tent like shadow puppets on canvas walls, and their movements are seamless, like close-eyed kisses. They are, only in my mind.

One time only.

The lights dim
and suddenly there's a spotlight
on center ring
and a man with words

                    d
                    r
                    i
                    p

                    p
                    i
                    n
                    g
from his mouth like gasoline.

"Come one, come all! To the world's biggest collection
of broken girls—
fire breathers that will take your breath away . . .
contortïonists that will twist your words
and leave you;
because leaving is the only thing they know how to do.

A traveling caravan!
Ladies and Gentlemen, boys and girls,
children of all ages . . .

See the brilliant;
the majestic creatures
that tread these tents with familiarity,
and here, they will always have a family."

i.

She hides her thoughts with a white mask
and a painted smile,
hopes and dreams of ever leaving
a place like this for somewhere better;
a dreamer amongst the broken dreams
of broken homes, and broken hearts.
She paints her skin
pearlescent
and leaves her imaginings
hung on a coat rack at the door
where she can pick them up, after the performance
whenever he decides it's over
and the torture of public humiliation
is exhausted.
She doesn't need to pain.t on fake tears;
tears in the very fabric of herself
are just that much more real.
And so she tattoos her words onto her skin
in hopes that someone in the sideshows

will stop to read them to her
like the lines in her palms
or the shade of her aura;
like the poetry she sometimes
allows to fall from the sky like snowflakes—
snow-white face paint
and a bloody grin.
She's here just to make you laugh again,
a piece of entertainment
to use at your convenience
and then
just throw away
and she will float away on a breeze
with your bruises on her lips.

ii.

A flash of rust,
a cloud of smoke;
a wildcat in the form of a girl
with knives for nails
and a poisonous tongue,
that could very well be
as sweet as cyanide.
She throws blades at walls
like breaking plates
and she bites her cheek
when she gets so close and doesn't.
Because she is trained to miss
every time.

It's all about the perceived danger
so false and superficial.
Her knives are dull
like aches and pains in her past-tense muscles
and she, she is waiting for the day where she will
sharpen her blades,
cut the ties,
and walk out
without the looming remorse
that comes with walking out on your family.
And she is not a practiced deadbeat—
just a practicing beatnik
dancing around her words
like the fire that sits on her shoulders.
She is a fiery soul
with eyes like earth and water
and hair like the wind.
She is beautifully elemental,
and she is smiling into the setting sun
that glares like an angry ringmaster
when his plans have fallen to pieces.

iii.

a.con.tor.tion.ist.
Twisting herself into fantasies
of men who want flexibility
in a relationship, without commitment
where they can come and go
as they please

and throw her away
when they're finished,
knowing she'll always be ready and willing
at three a.m. when they beckon her
with their lighthouse lullabies,
which do everything but help her sleep.
And she does not sleep;
she cannot with/out these grabbing hands
pulling at her clothing,
pulling at her hair,
pulling at her sanity,
when it is stretched so thin and fragile.
She was fragile
on the morning he caught her
trying to steal money from his wallet;
the littlest thief,
making runaway plans
that she kept hidden
knowing full well it was forbidden
to even think about leaving
when he's giving you
the only life you have known,
the best freedoms
and always at a price.
She paid for love
with something more than money
and it was as fake as her smile.

iv.

She's set on such a narrow path,
a tightrope walker
on someone else's fraying rope,
someone else's dying hope.
And should she falter, fall and shatter
to the ground,
and become the eggshells she walks on daily
when her weary feet are in need of resting;
or if the rope should snap—
like fingers at a poetry reading,
filling the air with sharpness;
if she were to go tumbling down like London Bridge
into an empty space, no netting
to catch her spirit
before it shatters
into a million broken smiles.
She looks for a safe haven here but
there is no home for this hummingbird
to rest her fluttering heart
and her aching wings
that will not save her when she's failing
so religiously with St. Anthony wrapped around her throat
like a last-minute promise
to herself
that she would stay sane
despite these canvas boundaries
that tell her
she is not to love
anything outside of t.his world

and though she wishes on a thousand stars,
she can never wish hard enough
to free herself from this
performance prison.

v.

They tell her to get off her high horse
but she can't help that the horse is tall
or that she feels powerful when she is standing
on its back, balanced like a top
where at any moment,
she could fall;
she is on top of the world
for just a second,
she is powerful for once in her life.
There's no stepfather to beat her senseless,
no mother to neglect her
as she cradles a bottle of Jack
instead of her baby.
She is not as skilled at equestrianism
as she is at just riding
and that is why he picked her up
convincing her that she would be a lovely addi(c)tion
to t.his mauled and makeshift family.
She came on her own free will,
as they all did,
praying for something better
than a hotel room home and a cigarette
when she knew

she'd just cough on the smoke anyway.
She is anything but shy
when displayed to a thousand hungry eyes
waiting to devour her talent
but behind the curtain of her d(ep)ressing room,
she is six shades of pink and shaking
more than just hands.
Shyly, more like a virgin than not
despite everything she's done;
despite everything.

vi.

She was a stoner,
a pebble,
kicked by the feet of a million,
whose rough exterior was never appreciated
or embraced.
She was constantly being worn down,
smoothed out edges
which made her words less abrasive.
She was a rolling stone,
who never lasted long enough to make a lasting impression,
just lit up and burnt out
like a cheap cigarette
hanging off the lips of a god with a grudge.
She was re.usable,
always able to be made into something new,
always able to be broken down
and built back up with his lust-laced tongue,

his dreamed metaphors and promises.
promises. promises. He promised her stability,
a job, a life working overtime for pen.nies
so she could write poetry in the corners of her eyes.
He made her into something,
something more precious than a petty stone.
He made her a diamond-
eyed star,
a many-faceted, Marlboro-smoking star,
juggling liars and make-believe martyrs
whose words she wore on her sleeves like broken hearts.
She juggles shadows and the demons
and the thoughts that float by on rainclouds,
she juggles the rain like teardrops,
throws them back up into the clouds.
.recycle.and.reuse.

vii.

She breathes flames
because she is truly no good with words
and she just needed something
to fill the empty space in her mouth
when she was tongue-tied and tired.
He found her skipping stones at the bay
trying to forget the music
her musician used to sing to her
in a time before time,
where even the sundials failed to change their shadows.
He heard her singing

a song between soft sobs
and offered to take away the memories;
replace them with something better,
all she had to do was take his hand
and follow his lead.
She wanders the rings like a ghost
with gasoline on her breath and fire in her words
hoping to burn anyone
that stands between her and Happiness.
And it was this that caused her to blindly burn her bridges
which were the only ways to escape Here,
where she will one day realize
she is trapped, caged; an animal
with a chained voice.
He is a Venus flytrap
setting out sweet promises
like honey
and devouring souls . . .
She longs for the bay;
for the skipping of stones at sunset,
where she could whisper to the sky,
"Be careful what you wish for."

The darkness is debilitating
and he will not raise the house lights
because he likes the idea
of his blind acrobats
falling at his feet
like stars;
real stars.

And when they hit the ground,
they feel around in the darkness
for the pieces of their shattered hearts
that have stumbled just out of reach
like a tumbling gymnast

and they,
they were all dreamers
taunted and taken advantage of
by a dreamcatcher's promise;
a man who knew
they'd spend hours on their knees,
praying for a way out,
to a god
he killed long, long ago . . .

He gathered up his girls
like poker chips
at the end of the evening
and tucked them into his pockets,
with a bedtime story
telling them,
"Tomorrow is another day."

Tomorrow is another day to suffer
in the presence of pseudo-saints.

He kissed each sparkling girl
on the forehead or the cheek,
promised them that morning
would come faster
if they just didn't sleep.

Blushing, Mild Disasters

You bring wildflowers to my skin
flushed red,
with every touch lingering
like a small catastrophe.

Landscapes

I want to learn the landscape of your skin,
your peaks and valleys
and where is best to catch the sunrise.

Games with Girls

He says, "It's like chess.
It's all about the strategy,
except with these wash-ups
it's all about the tragedy,
the bleeding words, the pretty herds
of poet girls who line my streets
for a chance to meet God;

a billion blind ballerinas
with twisted ankles and bruised egos
vying and dying for the opportunity
to serve at my feet
like little missionaries."

He says, "It's the way you smile,
my little angel. You're so beautiful . . .
Let me see your soul so I can teach you
how to fly. Let me meet your soul.
Take off your halo, babe.
It's trying to steal your gorgeous shine.
Take it off. Take it off."

It's the way his words encourage actions;
the way she fits in his plans,
because she is that one piece that is broken so right.
She tries to smile, holding fast to the idea of pleasing him
and how it will get her into heaven
one day, one day . . .

She told him she's not beautiful
while lying with her heart open and vulnerable,
clinging to the idea of creating something lovelier
than her thoughts could ever be.
And all she had to do is just pull the trigger.

He says, "I miss you,"
when she strays too far,
as if to guilt her into staying,
as if to tell her she's not leaving
and most days she won't,
because she feels so empty without him
there to draw her smiles.

But he's no artist,
and these smiles are just shaking lines
meant to tremble and shatter.
Like he wants her to,
and when she's broken down,
so weak and out-of-order,
she is his. And he is God.

God, why are you doing this?
What did I do wrong?

He says, "Babe, that's just the way
you play the game.
You take as many points as you can get,
no mercy—and when you win,
you move on to the next challenge;
the next little broken-hearted baby doll.

Sweet talk 'em and leave 'em bleeding on the floor
when they're too broken to play with anymore."

"It's like chess," he said.
"All strategy and staying two steps ahead
all the time. And when your queen has fallen,
you simply

give her up
and
move
on."

Narcissus' Girls

There are girls like her,
that perform purely for the reason
of not having to speak;
because their words are broken
so much like a record.

There are girls like her
and I just want to kiss their apple cheeks
and pray for them,
as they climb into speeding cars
going nowhere.

Girls like her,
steal my breath away,
those tiny, kleptomaniac mermaids;
I catch them reflecting in mud puddles
so shallow that they could never drown,
no matter how closely they resemble Narcissus.

Promises to My Synthetic Atlas

I promise to be the strength when you are tired
of holding up the world,
my synthetic Atlas,
with weary-growing shoulders.

I will be the ache in your limbs
and the beat of your bleeding heart
when you ruin your days
to see someone else's smile;

I will be the drive that pushes you forward
when you're so close to falling back.
I will be the pillar that you lean on
with sweat coated skin,
stretched over muscle and sinew;
a sweet smile and a tender kiss
at the end of a hard day.

I promise to be your favorite fantasy,
a too-good-to-be-true dream girl
to curl up in your arms when you are lonely
and in need of someone who understands
what goes on in your busy mind.

I will take the time to whisper *I love you* in your ear
after you've drifted off into some semblance of sleep,
lace my fingers in yours and trace the lines in your palms.

And when we are apart, I will think of you often,
every time I blink or notice
that my fingers are not curled around the fabric of your
clothing,
holding fast to you,
in case you were to disappear when I woke,
dissolve like the last sinking remnants of a dream.

I will write you letters of how much
I miss you, and how my body has memorized
the feel of your skin pressed to mine,
and how I miss the scent of you,
the warmth of your hands
when they're pressed against the soft parts of me,
my vulnerable-ness.

I will always miss you when I wake
and you are not the first face I see.

Stormsong

If thunder was as soft as your voice,
I would watch every storm
waiting for your laugh
like lightning.

Tally Mark Lashes

I, tremble terribly
      in the wake
            of your smiling eyes,
counting your lashes
      like tally marks
of how often I love you.

The Littlest Things

you are;
> the trembling in my fingertips,
> the sound of our beating hearts,
> laughter through a telephone,
> bodies lost in bedsheets

> &you are,
> promises on pillows,
> hope on bated breaths,
> and shivers down my spine

Quiescence

You are whispers written by sleeping thoughts,
traced on eyelids after I've sunk into slumber;
a place where I can dream of you
and memorize the shape of your hands,
your tired fingers, your work worn skin.

I remember you
when I wake, when I'm aching
for the thoughts of you;
for the sound of your voice,
your laugh, the way your words
curl into smoke when you smile.

A Memory, A Dream

Do you remember when we watched the mountain burn
from atop the school hill, where we used to sled
until our hands were raw and numb from the cold—
that was the night that I fell in love with your concerned
eyes.

How could they be anything but
when our lives burst into flames a thousand miles away,
we watched that mountain burn
like a stretching bonfire

and I held your night-raw hands tight against mine
as the townspeople crowded around us, screaming.
But you were the only thing in my snow globe world
that was real.

Do you remember when we watched the river rise,
creeping floodwater swallowing streets
and cars
and yards that filled knee-deep with rainwater.

Yes, we splashed in those puddles
that threatened to consume our sneakers
with muddy teeth

that night, the hurricane lapped our shore
and warned us river children to run for higher ground

but we sat on the edge of the streets as they filled with water,
throwing pebbles into overflowing rain gutters
and smiling into sunset,
and when the night kissed those rising waters
we walked the dry strip to the bridge
two miles down
to see the damage.

Yes, we've always been the kids to cope with tragedy
with love-worn hearts and a pack of matches;
we've always sat victim to disaster
and kissed danger until we were too tired,
too tired to fight anymore.

Yes, I love you.
I've loved you ever since.

Fast Paced and Frantic

I've always worn my vulnerability on my sleeve
like a shred of lace, always dodged and weaved my way
into hearts like a disease, or
a desperation.

I was a record song played low
on nights where the rain was its own song,
yes, I was a background vocal,
bleeding out, drowning in,
fading to black while the storm was singing
and there's no shame in that.

I was handwritten,
curled cursive like infantile question marks,
inked and smudged by the rain drops,
kisses; soft wet lips left me deaf,
left me black-and-blued, fountain pen poisoned.
I was a letter to a fine man,
closed-eyes,
tangled limbs
and *We can't do this anymore*s,

and I was a thunderstorm,
a crash and flash epidemic.

I was holding myself,
cross-legged and open-armed,

unarmored,
unable.

I was unstable.
Always, inadequate,
I knew myself better than any man
with a moleskin journal
and half a map to my mind;

a hassle,
a handful,
a hibernating heart
at a standstill,

I was a piece of a poem
broken off from a poet,
fracture-famous
and forgetful, forgettable,
forging friendships with lonely men,
a please, a tease
with tired eyes,
entire lines force-fed
down aching throats.

But what hurts the most
is how habit happens,
how harrowing the thoughts are
when I'm laid open as a casket.

Waywardly, Whimsical

Whimsy,
I have always kept myself in such a state of frenzy,
folded my arms like origami cranes,
and felt faithfully fanciful.

And alliterations, like pearls
dotted my neckline,
festering like flowers in the window-box
stretching toward the sun;

I was the one who always quoted queens
and queers, always wrote wonders
about the women who I made up in my head
like imaginary friends
but fragile.

Oh so fragile,

fragments of framed photographs
that I once I-spied with a camera lens
and these too-tired eyes;

these girls, these worlds
tied up together like my shoelaces,
knots of knowing we are intertwined,
eternally, except for the moments where
I remember I'm fall-

                              ing

faster than the rain,
it's almost September and almost something
that sounds like the end of a summer romance,
tastes like the time I bit my tongue to keep from screaming,

and this:
it's the same kind of ache in my chest,
like something burrowing into my breastbone
like a home, I'm home for someone's lost laughter,
someone's wishes in the midst
of a meteor shower.

I've always been a star,
six armed, silent when the night was young
and screaming when I shot across the sky
like a memory.
And I've always been just outside your reach,
always listened to your preach
from the back row of your brain.

I was whimsical, once
when all I wrote about was women with broken wishes
in bruised streets, ones that breathed out their turmoil
twisted their fingers through their hair
to remind me how much I hated myself.

Letters to My Someday Daughter

i.

There are words that bubble in the back of my throat
and I have a novel full of don'ts to tell my someday daughter,
hold her with scarred arms and tell her
of how the world hates
anything that can prove itself beautiful,
but tell her to be beautiful anyway.

ii.
There are men that will love you
only to hold you in their arms and kiss you and feel your
innermost thoughts as you whisper against their neck, but
there are also men that will twist your arm and spit words
that hurt your ego and hurt your heart. There are men that
will leave bruises around your eyes if you let them;
you must never let them.

iii.
There are scars that tell stories,
but you must never romanticize them. They aren't pretty,
they aren't interesting, but they mean you have hurt and you
are hurting and you have lived. It is okay to acknowledge
that. It is okay to ask for help. I never could. Please be
stronger than I was. Please be stronger than I am.

iv.

There will be parties. Please go to them. Please learn how to socialize and make friends so you don't end up so anxious that you can barely leave the house. Don't become your mother. Please go to parties, please make some bad decisions; try not to get into too much trouble.

v.

Learn how to self-soothe. Try not to rely on anyone if you can stand on your own two feet. Learn how to be alone and not be lonely; it will be your best strength. Read. Learn new words and use them frequently. Talk to people. Talk to me.

vi.

You will get sick, sometimes. You will feel pains in your spine and you will go to doctor after doctor, endure blood tests and needles and scans. Try not to lose hope. Try not to think about how much your mother hates needles or how she still cries at the clinic. You will get well, too.

vii.

Remember that I will love you.

> I love you.
> I love you.

Bruises on Your Neck Line

I am unsure of love,
of its strength, of its grip;
does it leave bruises when it takes you by the wrist
and leads you through the crowds that scare the breath
in your lungs so much that you have to force them out,
evict the air in your throat. Does it leave kisses on your
forehead
when you're fever-sick and sleeping off medicines you can't
pronounce
and can't even open, those prescription bottles
with these shaking hands.
You are elderly for a moment, at twenty-one, and you find
yourself
reliant on people who don't know you. But you're sick
and you're sinking. And you don't know love.

I am unsure of love,
of its voice, of its virtue;
does it sing those songs that you memorized in grade school,
lullabies that sound like the lilacs used to smell, before your
dad cut down the branches. It is simply a pile of stumps
and sticks. Does it scream when you're unstable, when
you're unwilling to work with anyone? And they'll call you
stubborn and they'll call you stupid. And even the rain
has something to say to the rooftop. At twenty-one, you'll
question everything.
You'll question nothing.

You'll wonder about the decisions you've made.
And nothing will matter.

I am unsure of love,
of its smile, of its teeth;
does it bite messages into your skin
in some sick adaptation of Braille or does it tell you secrets,
with its arms wound around your stomach
and its lips to the back of your head like a shotgun.
The sounds are deafening.
The sounds are a scared scream in an empty house.
The sounds are children laughing.
The sounds are commonplace noises blooming in the
sunset.
The sound of love.

The breaking of glass has never scared you so much as now.
And maybe it shouldn't.

Mazeltov.

Drifting

People drift.

I used to have thirty best friends, back when everyone was
a potential friend and there weren't enemies,
and I had places to sleep
when my parents were fighting about money,
and places to hide from the people who didn't want me
to succeed. But I lost half of them in custody battles
with ex-boyfriends and lost the other half as boys
who fell in love with me when I, myself, was unlovable.
And some of them picked up and moved
in the middle of the night
and didn't tell me
and left their beds unmade and their fridge
full of perishables.
And some of them fell in love
with each other
and forgot about me
and that was okay because I knew they were happy.

I used to have ten best friends, and people to protect me
from those who tried too hard to court me, from those that
didn't know that *no* was a real and valid word,
from those that pushed, shoved, and broke me
in lunch lines and were the reasons
I spent my school days hungry.
I used to have them, they used to watch me

pace a room with an apple in my hand,
and watch me exhaust myself in unhealthy workouts,
and walk home, and cry myself to sleep.
And some of them went to schools I couldn't
remember the names of and some of them moved to states
where I couldn't remember the time zones, and changed
their numbers and didn't answer e-mails anymore.

I used to have five best friends,
people to call mine
in a strange and foreign city where
I didn't understand the customs.
After all, I lived in a place without traffic signals,
and didn't know how automated crosswalks worked
or how people didn't stop their cars
to let you cross the street.

I used to have them, but we graduated college and hated
each other and now all there is between us is fake words
of missing each other and Facebook posts that you "Like"
but couldn't care less about. And some of them went on to
work in magazines and became semi-famous and started
selling their photographs to people who paid more than the
standard $12.99 that I sell on a day-to-day basis.

I used to have three best friends, who took me drinking
and celebrated and talked me out of trying the ecstasy
that I found on the bathroom floor in a restaurant that I
only went to because I had been dragged there. And they
protected me and carried me out of the bar when it was
raining and locked away my keys when I was stumbling-

drunk and unable to keep my eyes open and my mouth shut. I used to have them, they used to kiss me during drinking games and have seen me naked more than once and haven't yet complained about the way I cling to you until I'm sober. But we work separate shifts at separate jobs and I am the only one that's still miserable and available. And of the three, only two will acknowledge me in public and I'm too afraid to text the third.

I don't have best friends anymore. Not really. Not since everyone escaped this place and left me here, stuck in the very place I never wanted to be stuck in. But money is tight and rooms are expensive. And maybe one day, I'll have a healthy friendship. And maybe one day, I'll look back on the people I've loved and the people I've let shape me and wonder why we never talk anymore.

21 Things I've Learned in 21 Years

i. You must never remind a drunk of his dead mother,
unless of course, you like the feeling of him
crushing your windpipe beneath his thumbs,
unless of course, you like to fall asleep
to the idea that you may not get the chance
to wake up again;
the threat of he-could-kill-you-in-your-sleep.
Personally, I did not.

ii. You should never let your shoulders cave in;
you are not a coal mine. You are not a hole in the ground
capable of collapsing in on itself.
You are a diamond.

iii. You do not need to love every man or every woman that
you bring home to your bed. And chances are, they don't
love you either. Sex is fun, don't take it so seriously; you
never end up with the one you gave your virginity to anyway.
I didn't.

iv. Men will say you are a catch.
             Remind them that you are a trap.

v. There are lost people in this world. There are people who
hold eternities in their eyes and sadness behind their teeth.
They will want to be saved. You will want to save them.
You can't save them all.

vi. You are a body full of stardust.
You are a galaxy, immense and breathtaking and wonderful.
Never let anyone tell you you're less than that.

vii. You can't drink away your sadness
any more than you can eat your way out of a stomachache.

viii. You can cry.
                    People will stare.
                                        It doesn't matter.

ix. He doesn't love you.
It isn't the end of the world.
            Or maybe he does.
            And maybe it is.

x. Don't let on that you've a secret stash of money that you
keep in the lunchbox beneath your bed. Once this secret
is broken, the money disappears. Be humble, be kind, but
keep your wallet in your front pocket.

xi. No one knows the difference between being coy
and saying "No" anymore. If you say "No," mean it.
Do not smile. Do not laugh.
Your consent is not a game.

xii. Watch home movies.
Look at how you've grown. You're still growing.
You're always getting stronger. And even if you're weak,
you're getting better; remember that the flowers
must wilt to be reborn in the spring.

xiii. Let yourself be worshipped.
Worship yourself. Your body is your peace-place;
Let it sing with your soul song.

xiv. You are more likely to die of those prescription medications
the doctors say will help you than you are if you smoke a
little weed.
Remember that.
Have fun. Explore. Don't get in too much trouble.

xv. You are the world's most original novel.

xvi. Remember to eat. Remember you need water.
Remember to sleep.
I know it sounds silly but a lot of people
forget how to survive.

xvii. Rest often.

xviii. You should set goals for what you want to do.
If you never write them down, what are you working towards?

xix. You are never a mistake.
You are never a burden.
                    You are magic.

xx. Never let anyone steal your shine.

xxi. And remember that I love you.

                              I love you.

Remembering How to Forget

There are days where I remember how I felt
when my skin was open and bruised, barely
able to feel the difference between being abused
and being loved, hardly noticing that I was crying
and clawing at my ribcage, looking for a place
to hide within myself.

And curling up into the smallest
of balls, crushing my knees into my breastbone, and
the space where my stomach used to cramp
is now just a memory of his hands on my body,
the sunset spots on my thighs, turning red and faintly
yellow, fading into night-bruises.

There are days when I remember how it hurt to breathe,
and how I just wanted him to kill me;
how I never had the courage to do it on my own
but kept a pocketful of scars on my arms
and on my hips that told stories
of where the razors had been before
and after all this time, I cannot seem to remember
why I ever fell in love, and why on earth,
I'd ever try again.

Acknowledgments

Many thanks to everyone who had a hand in the making of this collection, whether a poem was directly about you, inspired by you, or how you made me feel inside. Whether you helped me edit, review, or read my work while I was still a closet poet, afraid of my voice. Whether you knew it or not. I appreciate you.

Thanks to my parents, Rodney and Patti, for backing me in all of my decisions and teaching me how to love; for appreciating (and sometimes squandering) my creativity; for always allowing me to be myself and make my own choices. Thank you for giving me the most solid foundation to build my life on.

Thank you to my sister, Amber, who has blossomed into one of my best friends and trusted confidants. I cannot imagine life without you.

Thank you to my teachers, my professors, and my instructors throughout the years. I would have never found my love of words if it weren't for your encouragements, constructive criticism, and kindness. A special thanks to Tracy Barcavage, Noelle Wayne, Lora Kerwin, and Kenneth and Kasey Campbell, without whom I would have never had the confidence to publish my innermost thoughts. A special thank you to the late Bob "Bobby G" Golding; my safe haven, my favorite confidant. You are forever in my memory.

Thank you to Colleen Miller, Julia Plale, Travis Hoffman, Jess Ross, Adam Steppy, and Rudy Davis for your friendship and support throughout the years. Many of you have been sounding boards, proofreaders, and sympathetic ears. Thank you to Anessa, Kristie, and Bethany, for your inspirations; you are a large part of my poetic personality. Thank you to Cory Concha, for your years of listening and review.

Thank you to Jessica and James, who have held my hand and guided me through the publishing process.

And finally, thank you to my boyfriend, Sam. You are my rock. You encourage me every day to be stronger and better than the person I was yesterday.

I would be nothing without any of you. I am truly grateful to have had the chance to be nurtured by each of you.

Thank you for your support.

About the Author

Kelsi Rose is a poet with over a decade of writing study and experience. She is also an award-winning photographer with a degree from Antonelli Institute of Art and Photography. Kelsi currently lives in Central Pennsylvania with her boyfriend, a quirky five-year-old, and her emotional support dog.